TATE TALKS

ANDREW TATE'S WISDOM UNVEILED

Introduction

Welcome to "Tate Talks," a journey into the mind of a warrior, a voyage through the triumphs, trials, and timeless wisdom that have shaped my relentless pursuit of success. I am Andrew Tate, and throughout my life, I've faced challenges head-on, conquered opponents in the ring, and built a life that reflects the unwavering determination to be the best.

This book is not just a collection of quotes; it's a glimpse into the mindset that has fueled my victories and inspired countless others to reach new heights. As you delve into these pages, expect to be challenged, motivated, and empowered to take control of your destiny.

Each quote is a reflection of my experiences – from the gritty training sessions in martial arts to the fierce battles in the business arena. "Tate Talks" is a testament to the belief that success is not just about talent; it's about cultivating a mindset that refuses to accept anything less than greatness.

Prepare to embark on a transformative journey. These words are not just meant to be read; they are meant to be absorbed, internalized, and used as fuel to drive you forward. Whether you're an aspiring entrepreneur, an athlete pushing the limits, or someone seeking the path to personal excellence, this book is for you.

So, let the journey begin. Open these pages, absorb the wisdom, and unleash the warrior within. "Tate Talks" is not just a book; it's a guide to conquering your world and living life on your terms.

Warrior up, and let's conquer together.

"Close your eyes. Focus on making yourself feel excited, powerful. Imagine yourself destroying goals with ease."

– Andrew Tate

"Find a person who is as successful as you'd like to be, ask them what to do, do it and work hard."

- Andrew Tate

"The temporary satisfaction of quitting is outweighed by the eternal suffering of being a nobody."

- Andrew Tate

"Your mind must be stronger than your feelings."

- Andrew Tate

"Absolutely every single one of my actions is intentional. Divine purpose. If your day is full of mindless action, you act without thought."

- Andrew Tate

"Success is always stressful."

\- *Andrew Tate*

"Freedom will only come when you no longer trade your time for money."

— Andrew Tate

"Cost is the enemy of the poor man, so the poor try to save money. Time is the enemy of the rich man, so the rich try to save time."

— *Andrew Tate*

"You must put in the effort to get the life you want."

\- *Andrew Tate*

"You are exactly where you deserve to be. Change who you are and you will change how you live."

— *Andrew Tate*

“Arrogance breeds complacency and complacency breeds failure.”

— *Andrew Tate*

"Do the impossible and you'll never doubt yourself
ever again."

– *Andrew Tate*

"The internet is the new battleground of earth, the wild west, the place of truth and opportunity."

— *Andrew Tate*

"Arrogance is the cause of most first world poverty."

\- *Andrew Tate*

"Today you can act as an amateur or you can be a professional. Decide what you will do right now."

- Andrew Tate

"Emotional control isn't a lack of emotion; it's a necessary function of maturity."

- Andrew Tate

"High standards protect you from low-quality experiences."

— Andrew Tate

"Aspire to be a superhero. Not a normal person with a bigger house and nicer car."

- *Andrew Tate*

"Intellect is nothing without energy. Ideas are nothing without energy. High energy people win."

– *Andrew Tate*

"The man who goes to the gym every single day regardless of how he feels will always beat the man who goes to the gym when he feels like going to the gym."

— Andrew Tate

"There is no joy without pain."

- Andrew Tate

"The amount of stress you can tolerate while remaining effective is directly correlated to the level of success you will enjoy."

— *Andrew Tate*

"Reject weakness in any form."

- Andrew Tate

"You can become rich, you can become strong, you can take care of your loved ones and enjoy the fact it will be very difficult."

— Andrew Tate

"No exceptional person ever lived
like an average person."

- Andrew Tate

"If failure makes you stronger, you can never lose."

- Andrew Tate

"The harder you work, the more important you become."

— Andrew Tate

"Show me a man with one friend and I'll see a man who's honest."

- Andrew Tate

"Don't listen to the advice of people who are living lives you don't want to live."

- Andrew Tate

"You are never going to have any of the things you want if you do not get them yourself. Nobody cares about you enough to do it for you."

- Andrew Tate

"Focus on what's best for yourself."

- Andrew Tate

"My biggest victories in life were when I was sad."

\- *Andrew Tate*

"I always win because I genuinely can't take losing."

- *Andrew Tate*

"The faster you work, the more work you get done."

- Andrew Tate

"Your only option to level up is to
begin talking to winners."

- Andrew Tate

"There is no light without dark. There is no joy without pain."

- Andrew Tate

"A man without a vision for his future always
returns to his past."

– Andrew Tate

"Searching for my favorite feeling has built me an
exceptional life."

\- *Andrew Tate*

"Stress tolerance is the best indicator of a person's likelihood of success."

- Andrew Tate

"Adversity builds men. It is your duty to challenge yourself and craft your own world."

- Andrew Tate

"You could be worth million dollars, and go into the war room, and go into a specific room, and the fact that you're worth million dollars will no longer matter. If you're sending a girl flowers, and she's going on a girls trip, then you will get shut down."

- Andrew Tate.

"They want to get rich, but they have no plan to get rich! And a hope and a plan are two different things."

— *Andrew Tate.*

"Money is always moving. If you get in the right place at the right time, then you're going to get some!"

- *Andrew Tate.*

"Money will fix all your problems. If money was so bad and did not bring happiness all the billionaires would be giving it away. Wake up."

– *Andrew Tate*.

"If you truly wanted money, you wouldn't be able to
sleep until you had it."

\- *Andrew Tate*

"You have to look at your business ideas and your plans, and find a way to remove your need for money to attempt the plan."

— Andrew Tate

"If you're surrounded by people who have a plan to get rich, and you provide value to them, sooner or later you're going to begin to make money."

- Andrew Tate

"I know more about making money than anyone else in the world. Most people's views on money are outdated. If you want to get rich in today's attention-based economy, then you need to learn modern methods of wealth creation."

- Andrew Tate

"A business is money in, and nothing else. It's not money out, it's not your account, it's not your logo, it's not your website, a business is money into a bank."

— *Andrew Tate*

"You will never get rich without a plan."

- Andrew Tate

"Your mindset is the single most important factor in determining your success or failure."

— *Andrew Tate*

"Success is not about luck, it's about having the right mindset."

– Andrew Tate

"If you want to be successful, you have to think like a winner."

- Andrew Tate

"The only thing holding you back from achieving your goals is your own mindset."

- Andrew Tate

"You are viewing yourself as a short man! Walk up and be THE man!."

— *Andrew Tate*

"A strong mindset is the key to achieving anything you want in life."

— *Andrew Tate*

"The most successful people in the world have a mindset of abundance, not scarcity."

— *Andrew Tate*

"The difference between those who succeed and those who fail is often their mindset."

— *Andrew Tate*

"Your mindset is like a muscle, the more you exercise it, the stronger it becomes."

\- Andrew Tate

"If you want to change your life, you first have to change your mindset."

– Andrew Tate

"I don't believe in motivation. I believe in discipline!
I am a disciplined person!"

\- Andrew Tate

"I don't need to be motivated because I'm disciplined. If I allocate X amount of time to do something, I'm going to do it."

— Andrew Tate

You're going to have to work when you don't feel like working. That's how it's going to have to be, or you're never going to be anything."

- Andrew Tate

"The temporary satisfaction of quitting is outweighed by the eternal suffering of being a nobody."

– Andrew Tate

"People who train every day do not want to train every day. They are not motivated to train every day. They have something else, they are disciplined."

- Andrew Tate

"Success is the result of discipline,
dedication, and sacrifice."

- Andrew Tate

"Discipline is not a punishment. It's a practice of self-control and self-mastery."

— *Andrew Tate*

"The difference between successful people and unsuccessful people is the willingness to do what others won't."

- Andrew Tate

"Discipline is the key to success. Absolutely is. If you cannot force yourself to do something that you do not want to do, how are you ever gonna put yourself through the suffering required for greatness?"

- Andrew Tate

"Discipline is the foundation of freedom."

- Andrew Tate